Tying Trout Nymphs
12 of the Best

Deke Meyer

Frank Amato

PORTLAND

Welcome To Tying Nymphs

Through step-by-step photos and description this book will show you how to tie the dozen best trout nymphs, some effective variations of the basic recipes, and some tips on how to fish these flies. Since it's limited to a dozen patterns, some favorites will undoubtedly be overlooked.

By definition, the term nymph refers to the underwater stage of insects before they hatch and become creatures of air and flight. Fly fishers often embrace other aquatic creatures under this description, including crustaceans such as scuds, shrimp or sow bugs. Some even include leeches. I've included a couple of these cross over "nymphs" because I believe the idea is to have fun and catch fish, so like many fly flingers, I lump various wet flies under this nymph-like category. It could be classified as a streamer, but I've tossed in the most effective wet fly of all time, the Woolly Bugger, because I believe no wet fly fisher should be astream or afloat without it.

Biologists estimate that trout feed subsurface about 90% of the time, so it makes sense to fly fish for trout in their favorite kitchen under the stream or lake surface. Armed with a selection of this dozen nymphs in assorted sizes you can catch trout wherever they swim.

This booklet attempts to give you all the information you need to tie these flies, but it can be very helpful if you can watch a friend, fly club member, or a fly shop person tie these flies.

Published in 1994 by Frank Amato Publications,
P.O. Box 82112, Portland, Oregon 97282.

Cover photograph: Jim Schollmeyer
All other photographs taken by Deke Meyer except *page 2*: Nick Amato

Softbound ISBN: 1-878175-87-4
Printed in Hong Kong

10 9 8 7 6 5 4 3 2 1

TABLE OF CONTENTS

Shopping for Tools and Materials

A supportive local fly club or fly shop is ideal and can prove to be a wealth of information. Mail order is workable if you get a knowledgeable salesperson via a 1-800 number.

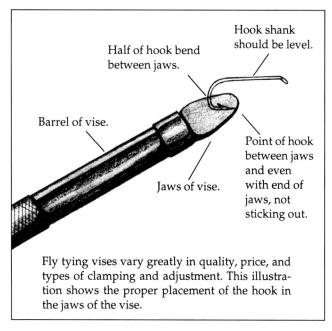

Fly tying vises vary greatly in quality, price, and types of clamping and adjustment. This illustration shows the proper placement of the hook in the jaws of the vise.

You need a fly tying vise, which range in price from inexpensive to very expensive, depending on workmanship and quality of the metals used. If you're on a budget, I recommend buying an inexpensive vise at first, then as you gain experience you will define your own preferences. Later on you can get a vise that will last a lifetime. You can use your first vise as a field kit vise or pass it on to another beginning tyer.

These Western March Brown mayfly nymphs exhibit the typical fuzziness of various underwater creatures with appendages such as gills, tails, legs and antennae. We tie nymphs to simulate that fuzziness, calling them "buggy". When tying nymphs, fuzzy is good.

Dubbing and Picker Tools

You can tie a tighter nymph by using a dubbing tool: make a loop with the thread, wax it, insert bits of dubbing between the two strands of thread that form the loop, twist the thread and the dubbing with the dubbing tool, then wrap the body. (See the Hare's Ear, page 17, Step 2; or Scud, page 27, Step 2.) Use a dubbing picker tool to tug out strands of spikey dubbing to make your nymph more "buggy".

Nymph dubbing includes spikey fibers that give your nymph a "buggy" appearance that might seem to a trout's eye such insect aspects as legs, antennae, nymphal gills, or other lifelike appendages. Use a dubbing picker tool with its miniature metal spikes to pluck at those protruding spicules, further enhancing your nymph's attractiveness.

You will need a pair of hackle pliers, scissors, bobbin, bobbin threader, dubbing tool and whip finish tool. Be sure to get scissors with finger holes that fit properly. Many are too small. A dubbing picker tool is helpful; or you can substitute a hacksaw blade or make a picker with the catchy part of a piece of hook-and-loop material (such as Velcro ®) glued to a piece of wood.

The most important component in fly tying is the hook. You can tie and fish with inexpensive hooks but you will miss catching fish because the steel is too soft and the hook is usually dull. The best hooks are chemically sharpened Japanese hooks—I recommend paying a little more and getting a whole lot more hook. After all, when you consider the amount of time and money you spend on tying flies, driving to the river or lake, and your investment in fly fishing gear, why scrimp a few cents on a hook?

How to Proceed: Tying the First Flies

You can buy hooks in boxes of 100 or in packages of 25. To begin tying these flies, you need a package of size 8, either 2x-long or 3x-long shank, and a package of size 12 wet fly hooks. You can add more hooks later.

Start with 3/0 thread, then go with 6/0 later. 3/0 is bigger so it's stronger, and better for cinching down material, but it builds up bulk too quickly. The smaller 6/0 thread is better overall; however, 6/0 thread breaks more easily. The traditional thread color is black, which is fine, but most tyers match the thread to the body color of the fly. Start with a neutral color: tan, gray or pale olive. (Some tyers who weight their flies with lead wire will tie the head with a specific color to denote a weighted fly, such as tying the head with red thread.)

Unlike dry flies, one advantage when tying many nymph patterns is that proportion is not as critical for the Woolly Bugger, Scud, Leech, Carey Special and others. In fact, "rough" often equates with "buggy", and trout seem to agree when they take our flies. Another advantage is that nymphs use less expensive hackle, such as rooster hackle that is not stiff enough to make dry fly grade. (Your wallet won't be stiffed for extra bucks, either.) Other inexpensive wet fly hackles include hen chicken, pheasant, grouse or partridge.

You can tie numerous wet fly patterns with yarn, or you can dub your flies. When you purchase dubbing, tell the shopkeeper that you want it for nymphs; nymph dubbing includes spikey fibers that give your nymph a "buggy"

appearance that might seem to a trout's eye to resemble such insect aspects as legs, antennae, nymphal gills, or other lifelike appendages.

Before tying, mash the barb down on the hook with pliers. (If you accidentally break the hook, you won't forfeit an already tied fly.) Most quality trout waters are managed for catch-and-release fly fishing with barbless hooks, but just as important, if you stick your clothes or your anatomy with a hook, it will easily come out. Always wear some kind of eye protection—you can lose your sight to a fly hook.

It might seem complicated at first glance, but fly tying is simply a matter of practice and proportion. My first nymphs looked as if they had ejected from the vacuum cleaner, only to be stomped by indifferent feet. But I caught trout with those unruly flies. With practice comes improvement, and trout eat imperfect nymphs.

I wish you enjoyable tying and fishing.

Attaching the Thread to the Hook

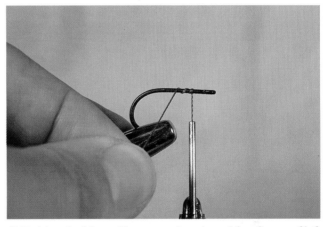

1) Hold end of thread between thumb and forefinger of left hand, wrap thread around hook shank with thread bobbin in right hand.

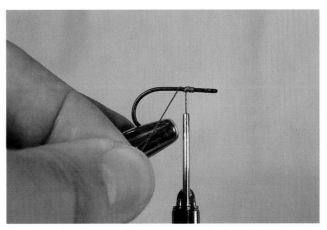

2) While maintaining light pressure on thread with thumb and forefinger with left hand, wrap thread back over itself with bobbin.

Nymph Tying Tools

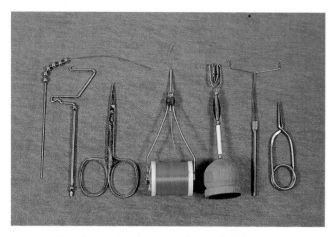

Besides a vise, basic tools needed for nymph tying include (from the left): bobbin threader/cleaner, Matarelli whip finisher, scissors, bobbin with thread, dubbing tool (two types shown), and hackle pliers.

The Whip Finish

Using a Matarelli whip finish tool is highly recommended because it is quick and easy to use once you learn how, and the head on the fly will be small and tight, making your fly more durable.

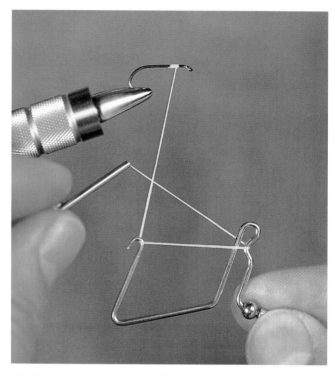

2) Allow tool to pivot on ball between thumb and forefinger: thread forms triangle, from head of fly, through tool hook, around tool bend, then back across in front of thread from head of fly.

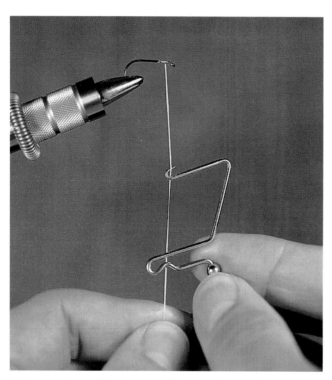

1) Grasp the tool by the small ball at the top of the handle between thumb and forefinger of right hand, thread bobbin in left hand. Tool hook goes around thread; bottom bend stays on your side.

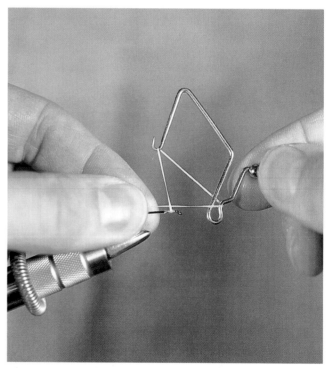

3) Allow tool to pivot on ball again, flipping triangle upside down and bringing triangle above hook, maintaining light pressure on thread bobbin. (The tool bend stays on the right side while the tool hook flips out towards you, ending above the hook shank, but still in a triangle.)

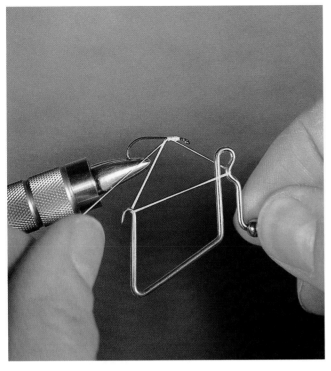

4) Keeping tension on the thread and allowing the tool to pivot on the ball, keep the tool bend to the right and wrap thread around the hook shank with the tool hook three times. (You still have the triangle, the tool hook flips out towards you while the tool bend stays to the right.)

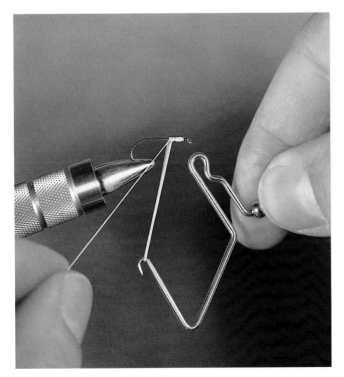

5) Maintain pressure on the thread and on the tool hook, tip the tool bend down until the thread slips off, leaving thread attached to the head of the fly and the tool hook.

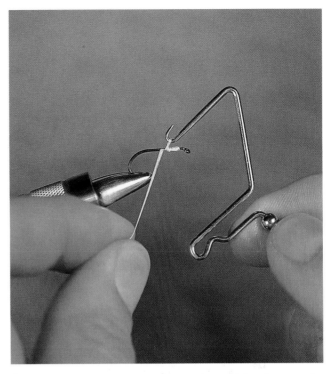

6) Pull on the thread while sliding the tool hook up to the fly head.

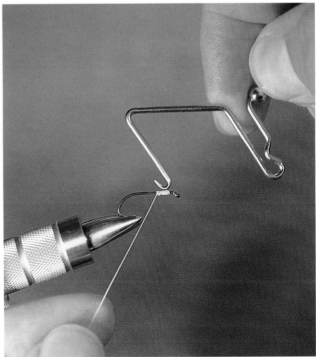

7) Tip the tool hook until the thread slips off, tightening the thread, which finishes the whip finish. (Instead of wrapping thread around the fly head six times (Step 4) it's better to make two complete whip finishes of three wraps each. It makes a tighter head and if the first whip finish breaks you still have a useable fly and one you can later add another whip finish.)

Bead Head Caddis

BEAD HEAD CADDIS

Hook: *Standard wet fly, size 8-16*
Head: *Gold bead, small*
Rib: *Fine gold wire*
Body: *Peacock, dubbing or sparkle yarn, olive*
Hackle: *Optional, mottled brown or olive soft hackle*

The "hottest" item in nymphing is adding a gold bead to standard patterns such as the Hare's Ear, Prince Nymph, etc. Besides incorporating light reflecting sparkle, a bead adds weight to the head of the fly, which helps to keep the hook from hanging up on the bottom.

This caddis imitation simulates free living caddis (Rhyacophlia) found among sunken rocks in riffles of trout streams. These caddis resemble segmented worms, ranging in size from 1/2 to 3/4 inch, in colors varying from tan to bright green. A common name for this caddis is the Green Rockworm. Olive is a good color for dubbing or fuzzy yarn, but peacock is my favorite because of its quality of reflecting bronze, brownish olive tones. The tiny hairs on the peacock fibers vibrate in the current, further suggesting a lifelike insect.

Tying Tips

I love the iridescence of a peacock herl body, but when trout teeth rake peacock it tends to break loose from the fly. You can strengthen the herl by twisting it around the tying thread, wrapping the body, then ribbing the fly with fine wire. Some tyers twirl the peacock around the wire, combining the rib with the body, wrapping it in one step.

Variations

You can increase the weight-forward aspect of a bead fly by wrapping lead wire around the shank of the hook, under the bead head, if the bead is the type that is countersunk.

You can make this a Caddis Bead Head Soft Hackle by adding two turns of mottled soft hackle, such as grouse, partridge, or hen hackle. This is biologically correct, because the Rhyacophlia caddis has six "arms" for grabbing its prey and to help it secure a hold on the underwater rocks. (A biological sidenote: they also sport anal hooks for anchoring themselves in the riffle.)

Another popular Rhyacophlia imitation is the Zug Bug: tail, peacock herl or sword fibers; body, peacock herl ribbed with tinsel; wing, mallard dyed wood duck color, 1/3 body length; sparse brown hackle.

Fishing Tips

These caddis make their living by eating other aquatic insects, so while they search for prey, crawling among the current swept rocks, some Rhyacophlia are tumbled downstream and eaten by trout.

Since this caddis is a worm that cannot swim, the best tactic is to dead-drift your fly along the bottom in riffles frequented by hungry trout. The next time you find yourself astream and ready to cast your nymph in a riffle, draw a bead on trout with your Bead Head Caddis.

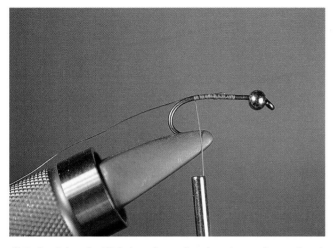

1) Debarb hook. Slide bead over hook point and up to hook eye. (You can secure bead to hook with Zap-A-Gap super glue.) Insert hook in vise. Attach thread. Tie in wire rib.

4) Wrap peacock rope to the front, tie off and trim.

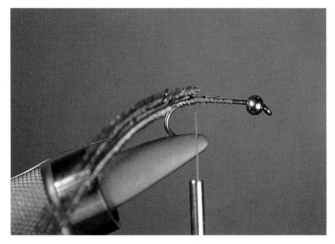

2) Tie in three peacock herls by their tips (go down a little on the herl; the very tip is too skinny and fragile).

5) Wrap rib forward in opposite direction, criss-crossing the peacock. (If peacock wrapped clockwise, wrap rib counter clockwise, or vice versa.) Tie down rib.

3) Twist herls around the thread to form a peacock rope.

6) Trim excess rib. Whip finish head behind bead and cement thread.

Carey Special

CAREY SPECIAL—Thomas Carey

Hook: 2x or 3x-long, size 6-10
Tail: Pheasant tail fibers
Rib: Optional, tinsel or wire rib
Body: Peacock herl, pheasant tail fibers, dubbing or yarn
Hackle: Pheasant rump feather

Tom Carey popularized the Carey Special years ago in British Columbia, but the Carey Special is now more of a generic pheasant rump soft hackle tied in various styles and color schemes. In somber tones of olive or dark brown it mimics a dragonfly nymph or small fish; tied in fluorescent red or orange it acts as an attractor fly, triggering strikes from large territorial predators such as husky trout. Like all soft hackle flies, the key to its effectiveness is the limber front hackle that readily responds to stream currents or your fly line machinations while lake fishing.

Tying Tips

You can reinforce the body with a wire or tinsel rib, which adds a reflective glint of light that suggests a living creature. To make the hackle easier to wrap, pull off the fluffy down-like fibers from lower part of the pheasant rump feather where the stem starts getting fat. Pheasant rump hackle's primary drawback is its fragile quality, causing the hackle fibers to break during casting, especially with the high speed line turnover we get with graphite rods.

Incidentally, that high line speed promotes wear on fly lines; even though they might look clean, microscopic particles cause abrasion while casting. To extend fly line life, frequently clean the line by pulling it through a soft cloth soaked with a vinyl protectant (such as Armor-All). Besides cleaning the line, the protectant invigorates the elasticity of the plastic line coating and helps keep it moist. A dried-out fly line will crack and absorb water and dirt and won't cast well. (For a sinktip or full sinking line, clean the sinking portion of the line via a soft cloth soaked in mild soap.)

Variations

Tying a Carey Special with yarn is the easiest and quickest method. You can use "buggy" yarns that exude tiny hairy spicules that add lifelike animation to your fly. You can use yarn with Antron or other light-reflecting fiber to gain additional lifelike iridescence. When tying smaller Careys, split multi-strand yarn, such as four strand, and just use one strand to reduce fly body bulk.

The most useful colors include black, olive, olive brown, brown, maroon, or bright colors such as red, orange, yellow or pink, and fluorescent shades. Tied without a tail or very short tail it simulates a dragonfly nymph or leech; trout might take a longer tailed Carey Special as a prey fish.

Fishing Tips

If you creep your Carey along, then make it spurt through the water you mime a dragonfly nymph. In a mountain lake I saw a salt and pepper colored dragonfly nymph do just that: after tiring of his pedestrian pace, he propelled himself quickly through the water by expelling water from his rear end.

If you impart a brisk stripping retrieve, you simulate a fleeing baitfish, prime prey for jumbo trout.

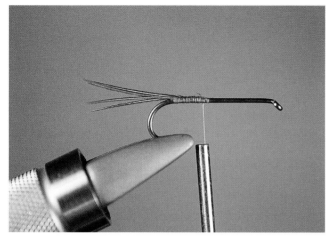

1) Debarb hook, attach thread. Tie in tail fibers, trim excess.

4) Tie in hackle by tip.

2) Tie in yarn for body. (By starting the yarn tie-down at the head of the body and working towards the rear, you get a smooth body.) Tie in rib, wrap thread to the front of the body.

5) Wrap hackle, tie off.

3) Wrap yarn forward, tie off and trim. Wrap rib forward, tie off and trim.

6) Trim excess hackle, whip finish and cement head.

Damselfly Nymph

DAMSELFLY NYMPH

Hook: *2x or 3x-long, size 10 to 16*
Tail: *Marabou*
Rib: *Optional, fine silver or gold wire*
Body: *Dubbing or fuzzy yarn*
Wing: *Tuft of marabou*
Hackle: *Optional, one turn of grizzly*

Damselfly nymphs are common on lakes and in many calm backwaters of streams, particularly on spring creeks. They are predaceous nymphs, feeding on other nymphs and small fish. Most have a year life cycle, crawling up a reed or plant stem to hatch in early summer, shedding the nymphal shuck, becoming an adult, mating, the female lays eggs, and dying by late summer.

Slender in body, the nymph is bright green, olive, or tan. The adult is most often a brilliant blue, sometimes bright green, flitting here and there, inspiring names such as the Blue Darner and Bog Dancer. We can forgive the damselfly its predaceous habits because besides providing food for trout, the adult is an efficient harvester of mosquitoes.

Tying Tips

The damselfly nymph reminds me of an aquatic praying mantis because of its slender body and long stick-like legs. Your fly should be slim, with a slim sprout of marabou for the tail, which is actually the damselfly's lungs. The nymph's three tails are used for sculling through the water and are filamentous gills. (That sculling motion is almost impossible to imitate, although I suspect the damselfly nymphs I've seen tied with a miniature plastic diving lip might do the trick.)

Variations

The most common damselfly imitations are tied in either bright green or olive. But don't overlook tan. The most common color of emerging damselfly that I've seen crawling out on shore, or most often, climbing up the side of my float tube, is tan.

Fishing Tips

Some of the most exciting lake fishing is during a damselfly emergence, when trout cruise the shallows with gaping mouths, intercepting the swimming damsels in gulping takes. If the nymphs are close to the surface you'll see a bulging swirl just underwater. When fishing the shallows, use a floating line and a slow hand-twist retrieve with pauses to fool fish.

If you fish a spring creek where nothing is hatching but there are backwater sloughs or reedy/weedy areas, slowly work a damselfly nymph along the edges of cover areas.

When damsels aren't hatching, searching a lake for hungry trout with a damselfly nymph in spring or early summer is still effective because trout often see damsels looking for their prey of smaller insects and miniature fishlets. Sunken weedbeds are excellent prospecting areas, because that's where damselfly nymphs live, and if you can find a weedbed close to deep water, you've found a good hunting area for jumbo trout because they prefer deep water nearby. Trout love to ambush damselfly nymphs and you will love it when a hunk of trout ambushes your fly.

1) Debarb hook. Attach thread. Tie in tail (1/2 hook shank length). Trim excess.

4) Dub body forward, leaving room for wing and head.

2) Tie in ribbing.

5) Bring ribbing forward, tie down and trim excess.

3) Wax thread. Spin dubbing by rotating dubbing and thread between thumb and first finger. (Rotate in one direction only.)

6) Tie in very short wing (1/4 hook shank length). Trim excess. Whip finish and cement head.

Fur Strip Leech

FUR STRIP LEECH
Hook: *2x or 3x-long, size 2-14*
Tail: *Continuation of rabbit strip wing*
Rib: *Medium or fine wire*
Body: *Fuzzy yarn or dubbing*
Wing: *Rabbit fur strip*
Hackle: *Optional, one turn of grizzly*

The freshwater leech is common in most lakes, some streams, and is not overlooked by foraging trout. The leech makes its living by sucking the blood and life juices from fish by attaching itself to the fish's skin, rending a hole in the fish, then feeding. For the leech, it's a case of eat, or be eaten by trout.

In form, the aquatic leech resembles the common worm. It's body is long and slim and it swims like an undulating string. Since it's difficult to imitate a swimming string, leech patterns simulate life and movement by incorporating rabbit fur, marabou, rough-dubbed fur, fuzzy yarns like mohair, and soft webby hackle into the fly. Generalist flies like the Wooly Worm and the Wooly Bugger may also be taken by trout as leech imitations. Black, dark gray, olive, and dark maroon are good colors.

Tying Tips

As with many flies, and particularly those designed as wet flies, you can't tie a lousy leech. As I've described it, you can picture the common garden worm, which the leech resembles, and you can picture its undulating swim through trout waters. Also, to aid its swimming, the leech contracts and expands its body. When you tie a fairly slender worm/leech fly, you imitate the leech. If your fly turns out bulgy and ragged, you may still have a leech pattern, or it may be closer to a dragonfly nymph or even a baitfish imitation. These types of flies simulate a variety of trout prey, whether trout take your fly for a leech or not.

In his book AQUATIC ENTOMOLOGY, 1981, Patrick McCafferty reports that leeches can get to 18 inches long. The most common size I've seen is more like four inches, and I've released trout that regurgitated black leeches about two inches long. So the most common sizes would be 6-10, 2x or 3xlong.

Variations

The most important variation may be taken as a leech by trout, or it may seem to be a small fish. The Marabou Leech is simply a reduced Woolly Bugger: retain the marabou tail and fuzzy body, eliminate the hackle palmered along the body. When retrieved, the marabou contracts and expands, undulating with your fly line manipulations. It's a very effective fly.

Fishing Tips

There is no bad way to retrieve a leech pattern. If you do it slowly, letting the fibers from the fur, yarn or dubbing react to your line movements, the fly simulates a leech. If your mood dictates that you need more motion in your retrieve, the quicker pace will emulate a small fish, prime food for big trout. Whether baitfish or leech, these maximum-movement underwater flies make suckers out of trout.

14

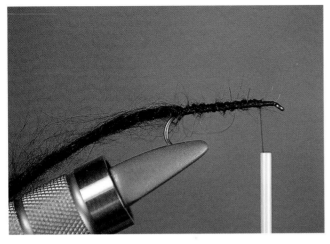

1) Debarb hook. Attach thread, tie in yarn at front of body, wrap thread to the back, then forward over body. (Leave enough room to tie down fur strip, wire rib, and head.)

4) Tie in fur strip at head of fly, trim excess. (Strip extends behind body, a hook shank length.)

2) Tie in wire, wrapping thread to the back, then forward, ending at front of fly (tinsel to the rear).

5) Secure fur strip by wrapping wire ribbing forward. (Moistening fur and guiding wire with needle or bodkin helps.)

3) Wrap yarn forward, forming body, tie off and trim.

6) Tie down wire at front of body and trim. Whip finish head and cement.

Hare's Ear

HARE'S EAR

Hook: *Wet fly, size 8-20 (12-18 most common)*
Tail: *Tuft of mottled fur or brown grouse feather fibers*
Rib: *Gold oval tinsel on rear half of body*
Body: *Blended mottled fur; light colored for rear 2/3 of body, dark colored fur for front 1/3; weighting optional*
Wingcase: *Turkey feather or other mottled feather strip*
Hackle: *Fur fibers simulate legs, antennae, etc.*

The true name of this fly is the Gold Ribbed Hare's Ear, originated in England by an unknown tyer. G.E.M. Skues, the father of nymph fishing, praised the fly in his book *The Way of a Trout with a Fly*, 1921: "I should like to know who was the genius who first conceived its possibilities, and how he got at his theory." Whatever its beginnings, many have since found the fly deadly on trout.

Traditionally, the fly used the fur from the ear of an English hare. Common usage has shortened the fly's name to Hare's Ear, and most are tied with rabbit body fur or other fur blends.

Tying Tips

The first key attribute of the Hare's Ear is the speckled effect derived from using mottled fur; most aquatic insects are not a solid color but exhibit mottled coloration. Secondly, not smooth like dry fly dubbing, the spikey nymph dubbing simulates gills, legs, and other aspects of aquatic insects. Rabbit and squirrel are the most commonly available mottled furs, made even more effective when mixed with sparkley Antron yarns.

You can simply dub the fur on the waxed thread and wrap it much as you would a dry fly, but a more effective method is using a dubbing loop. Make a loose loop of thread, wax it for better fur adherence, apply the dubbing to one side of the loop of thread, then with hackle pliers twist the threads and dubbing into a "dubbing rope". In his book *Tying and Fishing the Fuzzy Nymphs,* 1965, Polly

Rosborough called it a dubbing noodle, and in his *The Art of Tying the Wet Fly*, 1941, James Leisenring called it spinning a body. Using a dubbing loop tool is even better, as illustrated in the photos.

Variations

The standard Hare's Ear has a tan rear body and a dark gray front. Excellent variations include an olive rear with a dark olive front, or an all-black Hare's Ear with silver tinsel rib. You can substitute any dark colored feather strip for the wingcase, including duck, crow, or whatever you might find. A reduced version eliminates the wingcase; bring the rib only up to the end of the rear half of the body.

Fishing Tips

The Hare's Ear is fished subsurface, drifting with the current at the water level where the trout are feeding. This nymph is also effective in lakes, used with various retrieves, from slow to fast, interspersed with pauses.

When fishing a stream, the fly fisher's bobber, or strike indicator is helpful for detecting strikes to the sunken fly. An adhesive backed fluorescent foam pad or a piece of yarn works well. When a fish takes your Hare's Ear the indicator dips underwater and you set the hook. A simple but effective tactic for taking trout anywhere you find them.

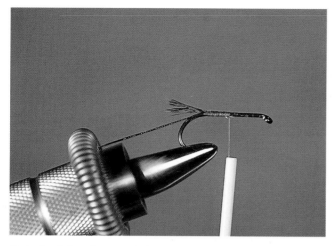

1) Debarb hook. Attach thread. Tie in ribbing. Tie in tail.

4) Wrap ribbing forward, tie off, trim excess. Tie in wing case material.

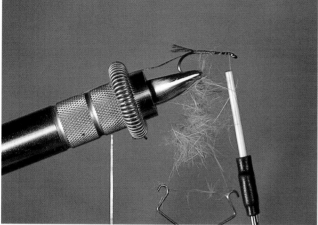

2) Make a loop with thread, wax thread. Insert bits of fur dubbing in loop, twisting thread to lock dubbing between the two strands of thread. (Photos illustrate use of dubbing tool which helps form the loop and twist the thread.)

5) Dub front 1/3 of body (as in Step 2 & 3), leaving room to tie off wingcase and whip finish head.

3) Wrap body up to 2/3 hook shank with dubbing.

6) Pull wing case over front of body, tie down, trim excess. Whip finish and cement head.

Micro Egg

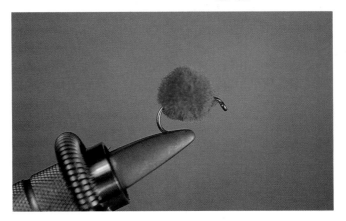

MICRO EGG

Hook: *2x-short, 2x-wide, humped shank or*
standard wet fly, size 10-16
Body: *Yarn ball or trimmed yarn*

As described in the Introduction, in our loose definition of nymphs as wet flies, instead of the egg-laying cycle of aquatic insects, we're going to include that of fish. I remember the story Jack Hemingway tells about being teased by his fly fishing cronies about using maggots for bait.

"Maggots are nymphs because they are the immature form of flies", he replied.

By fishing these micro eggs you can subscribe to the theory that your egg fly imitates the immature form of fish, many of which are similar in size to aquatic insects, and you'll be fishing a standard nymphing dead-drift tactic. Trout don't care—they eat eggs or bugs.

Tying Tips

As illustrated in the photos, there are two ways to tie a micro egg. The most straightforward method is to purchase round yarn balls at a craft shop or department store. These round acrylic yarn balls are bound in the center with thread or wire. They come in a variety of sizes and colors such as pink, white, red and fluorescent orange. Use Zap-A-Gap to super glue the yarn ball to the hook. It's waterproof and designed to fill in gaps between the bonded materials.

Because they reduce snag-ups but still hook fish well, for micro-eggs I prefer extra-short humped-shank hooks marketed as caddis larva, shrimp or grub hooks, such as the Tiemco 2487 or the Daiichi 1130. The 2x-heavy wire of the Tiemco 2457 is an advantage when fishing rivers with large fish, such as the Deschutes with its prowling steelhead. Of course, you can also use a standard wet fly hook.

The 3mm micro-egg matches a size 16 grub hook, the 5mm matches a size 14 grub hook, and so on.

The second method is to tie in lengths of yarn, then trim them to a round shape. Because you will be exerting pressure to secure the yarn, use heavier tying thread (3/0 or stronger). Some colors of bright tying threads of thick diameter match the fluorescent yarns available.

Variations

Although fish eggs exhibit a pale translucent hue and measure a little over 1mm in diameter, I've had excellent success with fluorescent orange, pink and red egg flies of 3, 5, and 7mm in diameter. Perhaps their success stems from an inherent attraction factor—the same factor at work when steelhead and fresh Pacific salmon take brightly colored egg patterns, biting egg flies long before they begin spawning. To some extent the color factor remains a mystery.

Fishing Tips

Tactics are simple: keep your egg dead-drifting close to the bottom. Because these yarn eggs are neutral density, fine tune your drift with micro shot. Stay alert for the take of the fish. Your strike indicator will only dip a bit, or pause in the current; when in doubt as to whether it's a strike, go ahead and set the hook. You don't need a huge yank on the rod, merely lift the rod tip to hook the fish. If it's not a fish, lower the rod tip and continue the drift with minimal disturbance.

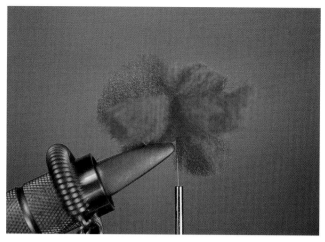

1) Debarb hook. Slide yarn ball over hook. (Insert hook through center of thread or wire loop in center of yarn ball.) Clamp hook in vise, leaving yarn ball to the rear. Put one drop of super glue on hook, in center.

2) Slide yarn ball onto glued area.

Method Two

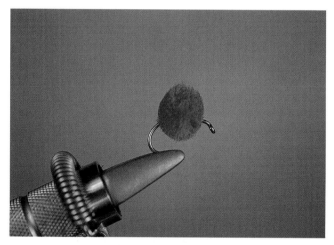

3) Debarb hook. Attach thread at hook center. Tie in one-inch length of yarn in center, on top.

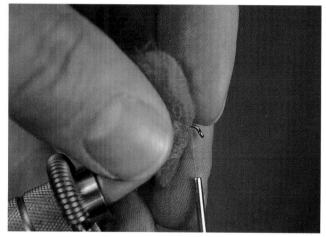

4) Tie in three additional lengths of yarn in center: on the bottom and both sides.

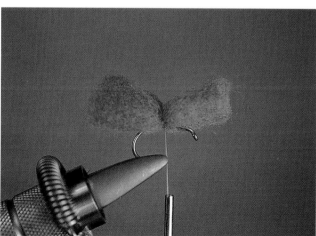

5) Pull yarn out of way, bring thread forward, in front of yarn, make two wraps.

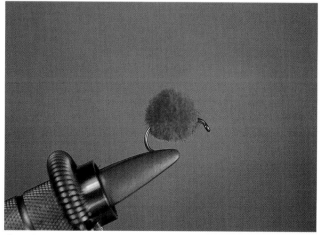

6) Whip finish and cement thread. Take yarn/hook out of vise and trim to round shape. (Egg fly back in vise for photo purposes.)

Montana Stone

MONTANA STONE

Hook: *2x, 3x, or 4x-long, size 4-10*
Tail: *Black fiber hackles*
Underbody: *Lead wire*
Body: *Black chenille or yarn*
Thorax: *Yellow chenille or yarn*
Wingcase: *Black chenille or yarn*
Hackle: *Black*

The Montana Stone was obviously first flung on the waters of Montana where giant stoneflies hatch in abundance, causing trout and trout fishermen to go crazy. The Salmon Fly (Pteronarcys californica) hatches throughout the West, getting its name from the adult's salmon-flesh colored underbody. In Colorado it's called the Willow Fly because the adult stonefly clambers about on streamside willows.

The Montana Stone is a prototype nymph, however, because you can change the pattern's size and color to match the Golden Stone or the tremendous numbers of smaller stoneflies that hatch throughout the season all over the country.

Tying Tips

It matters little to the trout whether you use chenille or yarn to tie this fly; both are effective, inexpensive, and come in a variety of colors. Split multi-strand yarn for small stoneflies; use thinner or fatter chenille depending on the size stone you tie. Saddle hackle dyed black is less expensive hackle material and works well.

Variations

Since this prototype can match a myriad of stoneflies, ask anglers or fly shops local to the rivers you plan to fish as to the size and color of the prevalent stonefly nymphs. An effective variation is the Golden Stone, tied with a brown body, yellow thorax and brown hackle and tail.

Realistic stonefly imitations abound, tied with special dubbing, elaborate wingcases, and intricate legs, antennae and tails. In fact, advanced tyers challenge themselves with stoneflies tied so bug-like, the nymph looks as if it might walk off the tying bench. These model insects look great in frames as mounted displays of fly-tying-as-art. However, if you want to catch trout, sometimes simple is better, particularly if your stonefly nymph is bouncing along the bottom of a rock infested trout stream.

Fishing Tips

Since the natural stonefly nymph spends its life on the bottom of the river, that's where you must present your fly. Although the Montana Stone is most often tied with a lead wire underbody, when fishing you will probably need to add micro shot to your leader to get the fly to drift close to the bottom of the stream.

As an interesting biological note, the Giant Stonefly browses on miniature aquatic growths; however, the Golden Stone is an active predator, eating smaller aquatic insects of all types. The ecological irony is that, in turn, trout pounce on stoneflies. We pose the final irony when we trick trout with nymphs replete with sharp hooks disguised within fly tying materials, pouncing on trout to land them.

1) Debarb hook. Attach thread, wrap thread length of hook, ending at rear of body. Wrap lead wire around shank, covering middle 3/4 of body (leave room to tie in tail and head). Wrap thread forward over lead, then back to rear of body. Tie in tail hackle fibers (1/4 body length), trim excess. (To better tie in chenille, strip fuzz from last 1/2 inch of chenille by stripping it between your first finger and thumb, then tie in core.)

4) Tie in 3-inches of thorax chenille, wrap forward, tie off and trim. (Leave room for hackle tie-down and head.)

2) Tie in 4-inches of chenille so fat fuzzy part starts at end of body. Wrap chenille forward to 2/3 hook shank, tie off and trim. (To get a less bulky tie-down with chenille, take two or three wraps of thread over the chenille to tie it down, placing your thread wraps over each other, at the end of the body. Cut the chenille, leaving 1/4-inch extra. Strip the fuzz from that extra bit using your fingernails or tweezers. Then tie down the core.)

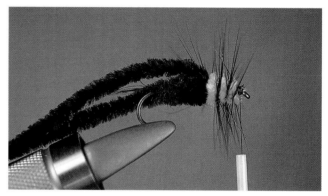

5) Wrap hackle through thorax, space wraps apart. Tie off and trim.

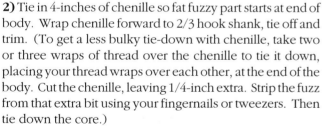

3) Tie in hackle. (See Prince Nymph, page 25, steps 4 & 5.) Tie in two strips of body chenille, each 3-inches long.

6) Bring two chenille strips over top of body, forming wingcase, tie off, trim excess. Whip finish and cement head.

Pheasant Tail

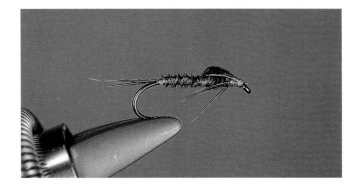

PHEASANT TAIL

Hook: *Standard length or 1x-long wet fly, size 12-20*
Tail: *Chinese ringneck pheasant tail fibers*
Rib: *Fine copper or gold wire*
Abdomen: *Rear part of the body; twisted fibers from tail of Chinese ringneck pheasant*
Thorax: *Front part of body; twisted fibers from tail of Chinese ringneck pheasant*
Wingcase: *Fibers from tail of Chinese ringneck pheasant*
Hackle: *Fibers from tail of Chinese ringneck pheasant*

As you might suspect from the name of the fly and its components, this fly requires only a hook, a bit of wire ribbing, and a Chinese ringneck pheasant tail feather. This simplistic pattern comes to us from the British Isles, where tyers made use of feathers from sport-shot estate pheasants. This fly incorporates the mottled brownish reddish coloration common to mayfly nymphs in England and the US, and is particularly effective on spring creeks. The pheasant fibers provide a fuzzy outline that may suggest a "bugginess" to trout, further enhanced by the glint of reflected light from the wire rib.

Tying Tips

Besides the coloration, the key to an effective Pheasant Tail is its slim profile. Many mayfly nymphs exhibit that slender contour, so when tying the Pheasant Tail, keep it svelte. The tail should be short, and the front hackle fibers are also few and short, merely suggesting legs. Put three fibers on each side of a size 12 or 14, two fibers on each side of a size 16, one on an 18 and none on a size 20. Some eliminate legs on size 18.

To strengthen your Pheasant Tail, wrap the wire opposite the direction you wrap the feather fibers; if you wrap the fibers clockwise, wrap the wire counterclockwise. Criss-crossing plasters the fibers to the hook, especially when sharp fish teeth scrape the feather fibers. You can twirl the fibers around the thread when you wrap the body, which makes the fly messier, but stronger.

Variations

The most effective variation is a reduced version: substitute peacock herl for the front part of the body; eliminate the wingcase and legs. Then bring the wire rib up to the head, reinforcing the peacock herl.

You can tie the Pheasant Tail with feathers dyed black or olive. I'm not sure what the all-black Pheasant Tail represents to trout (they don't talk much) but it must seem like some kind of food because they bite it. I suspect it mimics a drifting midge pupa, which are often black.

The olive Pheasant Tail emulates olive brown mayfly nymphs that dwell in most trout streams. Another effective variation is to tie the Pheasant Tail with a mix of olive and natural undyed feather fibers, imparting an mottled brownish olive shade, a convincing color to feeding trout.

Fishing Tips

Because trout take a trim Pheasant Tail well, spring creek fishermen use this fly when trout aren't working on top. Size 18 is the most effective size for spring creeks because there are always a few mayflies of that size within range of trout teeth. Because of its slim profile, the fly is not weighted. To get it down to the fish, use non-toxic micro shot, fine tuning the amount of weight needed for a good drift.

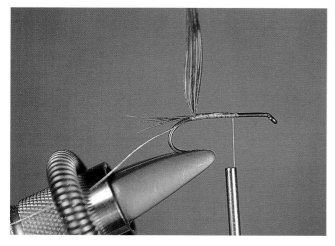

1) Debarb hook. Attach thread. Tie in tail (1/2 body length), trim excess. Tie in ribbing. Tie in feather fibers for body. (Tie in fibers by tip.)

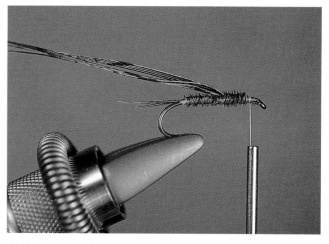

4) Tie in fibers for front 1/3 of body and wrap front of body (as in step two), leaving room to tie off wingcase and whip finish head.

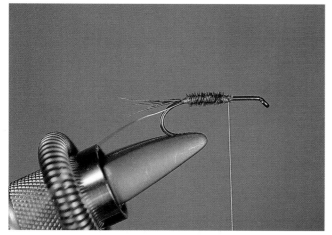

2) Wrap body up to 2/3 hook shank with fibers and trim.

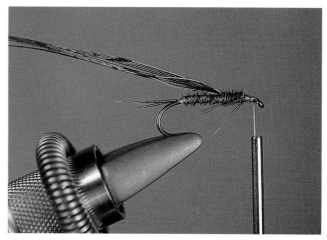

5) Tie in leg fibers on both sides (wingcase length) and trim.

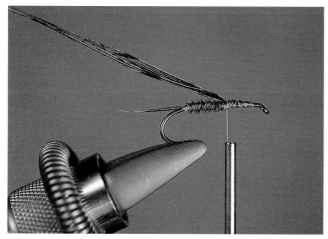

3) Wrap ribbing forward, (in opposite direction, to crisscross body fibers), tie off, trim excess. Tie in wing case fibers.

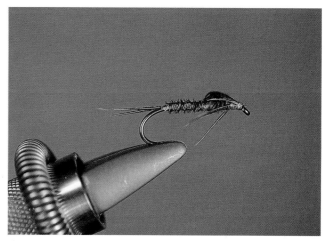

6) Pull wing case over front of body, tie down, trim excess. Whip finish and cement head.

Prince Nymph

PRINCE NYMPH—Doug Prince

Hook: *2x or 3x-long, size 8-16*
Tail: *Brown goose biots*
Rib: *Fine gold wire*
Body: *Peacock herl*
Wing: *White goose biots*
Hackle: *Brown*

The dressing for the Prince Nymph has changed some since Doug Prince introduced the fly sometime around 1940. This version is the most widely used, honed by zillions of hours at the end of fly lines by fishermen and guides.

What the fly imitates is hard to say—I'm not aware of any subsurface aquatic insects with slender white wings. We can speculate, however: the short brown tails mimic those found on some stoneflies and mayflies; the white wings simulate the white body stripe found on a few mayfly nymphs, or they suggest caddis nymph wings, or the striped coloration of a few small fish.

I believe one key to the fly's success is the peacock herl body. Peacock herl fibers seem iridescent in sunlight, reflecting bronze, brown, red and green tones of light, and not as a solid color, but mixed hues. Since nymphs are not a solid color, but mixed gradations of color tones, the peacock suggests that mixing. If you subscribe to the theory that fish look for specific aspects of prey to trigger a strike, such as a blend of color, then peacock is an advantage. Also, the hairs on the peacock fibers vibrate with every little whim of current in a stream or with each twitch imparted to the fly line when lake fishing.

To some extent the brown hackle imparts a bit of lifelike movement when activated by river currents or line manipulation, but I've seen anglers catch fish with Prince Nymphs tied without hackle. When the Prince loses its wings, however, the fly loses its trout appeal. Whatever the trout see in those white wings, without them the fly is not nearly as effective.

Tying Tips

If you just ran out of Prince Nymphs as a friend of mine did while fishing a trout lake infested with toothy cutthroat and submerged brush, both of which decimate flies, you can tie and fish a reduced Prince. Eliminate the wire rib and the front hackle, particularly in size 14 and smaller.

Variations

Although you could consider it a variation in that it uses peacock herl for the body, the Halfback is actually a different fly. The Halfback recipe: brown hackle fiber tail, peacock body, mottled brown feather fibers for the short wing, brown hackle. An excellent fly for trout wherever they swim.

Fishing Tips

To catch trout, these peacock nymphs can be dead-drifted in streams or animated with a hand-twist retrieve in lakes. You can swim your nymph downstream just a little faster than the current and fool trout that reject the standard free drifting fly. I suspect the iridescent liveliness of the peacock makes trout react to a swimming nymph getting away from them; as competitors with other trout for food, they react by eating your peacock nymph.

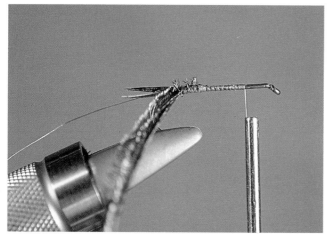

1) Debarb hook. Attach thread. Tie in short brown tails on edge (1/3 body length). Trim excess. Tie in three peacock herls by their tips (go down a little on the herl; the very tip is too skinny and fragile). Tie in rib. Bring thread to front of body.

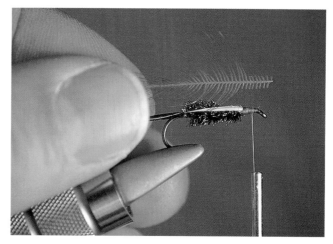

4) Select hackle so width equals 1/2 body length. (Gently stroke hackle down from tip so it stands out for sizing.) Trim hackle fiber stubs for more secure tie-down.

2) Wrap peacock herls forward, leaving room for wings, hackle and head. Tie off, trim excess. Wrap rib forward, tie off, trim excess.

5) Tie in hackle, with shiny side to the outside, towards you.

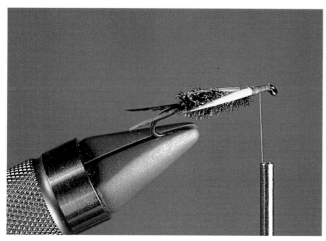

3) Tie in wings, flat over body, "V" shape (to just shy of body length). Tie off, trim excess. (In photo vise turned slightly to give you more of a top view.)

6) Wrap hackle two to four turns, tie off. Trim excess hackle, whip finish and cement head.

Scud

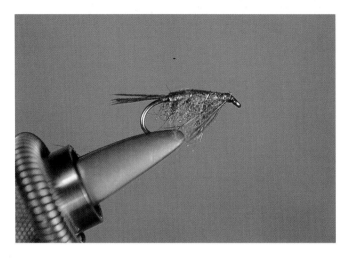

SCUD
Hook: *Wet fly, size 8-20*
Tail: *Short tuft of fur or hackle fibers*
Rib: *Fine silver or gold wire*
Body: *Rough dubbing, picked out*
Shellback: *Clear plastic*
Hackle: *None, or short hackle fibers*

The scud is a scavenger, picking over living and dead aquatic plants and insects. As a crustacean it's related to freshwater shrimps and sowbugs, and even crayfish. From a fly fishing viewpoint, you can simulate scuds, sowbugs and shrimps with the same rough-dubbed "buggy" pattern in a range of sizes and colors.

These unassuming critters inhabit almost all streams and lakes, and feature regularly in trout menus in stillwater. Scuds and such are fond of shallow water areas with submerged plants, which also attract trout because of the variety of nymphs present.

Tying Tips

You really can't tie a bad scud. If it turns out raggedly, scraggly and not exhibition quality, you've just tied an excellent scud, shrimp or sowbug. These creatures have some type of shellback or carapace, and bounteous legs or leg-like appendages extruding from their bodies. They are not tidy and neither is the fly that mimics them.

You can use coarse yarn to tie this fly, but I've never found any of the right color or "roughness". For dubbing, use a coarse blend with plenty of guard hairs. You can wax your thread with extra sticky wax, then dub the body, but too many of the hairs will be bound down to the hook.

A dubbing loop provides a secure hold on the hook, while allowing the guard hairs to protrude out from the body of the fly in all their glory, reacting to the slightest fly line manipulations. You can enhance the "bugginess" of your fly by plucking at the hairs with a "dubbing picking tool", which is a needle armed with wire hairs that catch the dubbing and pull at it. You can substitute a hacksaw blade or make a picker with the catchy part of a piece of hook-and-loop material (such as Velcro ®) glued to a piece of wood.

Variations

Like most underwater critters, these crustacea match the overall coloration of their environment as a protective camouflage. If the water they swim is fairly clear, they will exhibit a pale gray coloration; if the water has an olive brown cast to it, the bug will show that coloration. Fly fishermen catch trout on pink scuds, which imitate dead scuds, but even deceased they must be tasty to trout palettes. The most common colors I use are gray, grayish olive, olive brown and pink, in sizes 10 to 18.

Fishing Tips

When motoring through the water, scuds scoot at a snail's pace—very slowly. Use a dead-drift presentation in a stream; a mite faster in lakes, such as a slow hand-twist retrieve. Fortunately, this fly is quick and easy to tie, so you won't hesitate to work it among the sunken brush surrounding your favorite trout lake—which is also a favorite place for trout to snack on scuds.

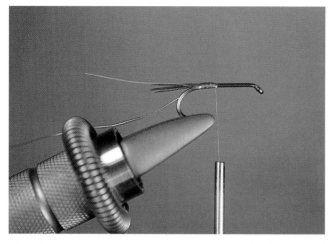

1) Debarb hook. Attach thread, tie in tail tuft, ribbing and shellback.

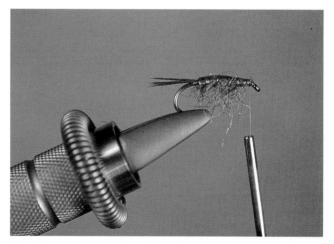

4) Tie off dubbing and trim excess.

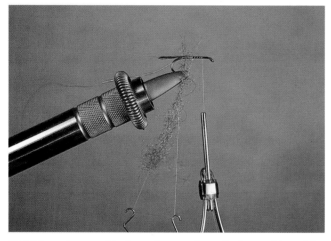

2) Make a loop with thread, wax thread. Insert bits of fur dubbing in loop, twisting thread to lock dubbing between the two strands of thread. (Photos illustrate use of dubbing tool which helps form the loop and twist the thread.)

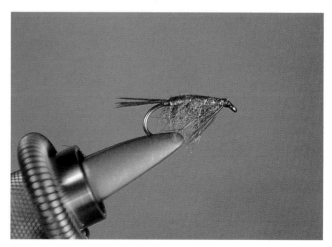

5) Pull over shellback and tie down. Trim so it covers just the top and a little of the side of the body. Bring ribbing forward, tie down and trim.

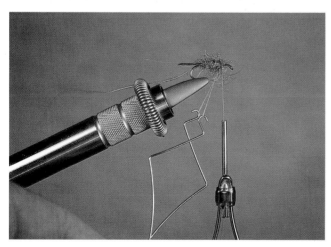

3) Dub fat body by wrapping dubbing forward. Leave room for shellback and tinsel tie-down, optional front legs, and head.

6) Tie in and trim optional front legs if desired. Whip finish and cement head.

Soft Hackle

SOFT HACKLE

Hook: *Dry or wet fly, size 8-20 (12-18 most common)*
Tail: *Optional, same as hackle*
Rib: *Optional, fine gold, silver, copper wire or tinsel*
Body: *Dubbing or fine yarn*
Hackle: *Soft flexible webby hackle: grouse, partridge,
hen chicken, pheasant, etc.*

The Soft Hackle is not a specific fly but a type of fly. It's chief characteristic is the flexible webby hackle that undulates in the water with every little whim of the current. The Soft Hackle dates to the very beginnings of fly fishing:

In one of the first written works on fly fishing, Dame Juliana Berners *A Treatise On Fishing With A Hook*, 1496, wrote: "And the following are the twelve flies with which you shall angle for the trout and the greyling and make them as I shall now tell you. The dun fly. The body of dun wool and the wings of the partridge. Another dun fly: the body of black wool and the wings of the blackest drake, and the feathers of the jay under the wing and under the tail."

In *The Practical Angler*, 1857, W.C. Stewart wrote: "The hackle generally plays a very conspicuous part in the construction of trouting flies. We think the cock-hackle by no means deserving of so much attention as is bestowed upon it, being too stiff and wiry to represent the legs of an insect, and we prefer hen-hackles, or still better, the small feathers taken from the neck or outside of the wings of a variety of small birds."

Tying Tips

The soul of the Soft Hackle is simplicity itself. I've had great success with Soft Hackles tied with no tail or ribbing, just a slim body of dubbing or slender yarn, and two turns of hen or grouse hackle. Finding hackle that is sized to smaller hooks can be a problem; the photos show how to tie flies with hackle that would otherwise be too big.

Variations

I've used Soft Hackles with the overall coloration of tan, creme, yellow, olive and gray in streams and lakes with great success. Sometimes fish will show a preference for a color tone that matches a hatching insect and sometimes they prefer Soft Hackles without tails. Tying them in a variety of sizes and colors will increase your chances for success.

Fishing Tips

Fishing the Soft Hackle is quite simple: cast it across the stream and let it swing back towards you. Trout often nail it when it swings across in front of them. With field experience you will learn how to mend your line to slow the cross current swing down, more readily imitating a swimming insect (most insects swim slowly). When fishing a lake, try varying your retrieve from slow to fast, and intersperse pauses.

I've also had great success on hard-fished waters with Soft Hackles that float in the surface film or just under it in a dead-drift, much like a hatching natural insect. However, be prepared, because trout don't take Soft Hackles softly, but with a hard strike.

1) Debarb hook. Attach thread. Wax thread. Apply dubbing to thread, spinning thread and dubbing together.

2) Wrap dubbing to 3/4 hook shank. Tie in hackle by butt, shiny side up. (Leave fiber stubs for tie down, see Prince Nymph, page 25, steps 4 & 5.) Soft hackle width should approximate hook shank length but it's not crucial, as in a dry fly.

3) Secure feather stem at the tip with hackle pliers, then moisten and stroke hackle to the rear.

4) Wrap hackle, trim excess. Whip finish and cement head.

Method Two for Oversize Hackles

5) Size soft hackles that are too long so that when tied down they approximate hook shank length. Distribute soft hackle around tie-down spot, securing with thread, so that soft hackles radiate to the rear from all "sides" of the fly.

6) Trim excess hackle from head area, whip finish and cement head.

Woolly Bugger

WOOLLY BUGGER
Hook: *2x or 3x-long, size 2-14*
Body: *Yarn, chenille or dubbing*
Hackle: *Palmered, usually natural or dyed grizzly saddle tied in by tip*
Tail: *Marabou, same color as hackle; added strands of Flashabou or Crystal Flash optional*

Some good color combinations include (body/hackle): black/grizzly; black/olive; black/fluorescent blue with blue Flashabou in tail; brown/grizzly; brown/olive; brown/ brown.

Tying Tips

Some tie the Woolly Bugger without a lead wire underbody, theorizing that the fly has a smoother underwater movement and reacts better to the angler's fly line manipulations. The advantage to lead weighting is that the fly sinks better, and if you weight just the front of the fly as in the photos, the fly exhibits an up-and-down jigging effect on the retrieve, which attracts big fish. There is no "right" or "wrong" way to tie this fly. Also, marabou "shrinks" when underwater, so tie in about twice the amount you want the sunken fly to display. However, too much marabou inhibits the sink rate of the fly.

Variations

The origin of the Woolly Bugger lies with the Woolly Worm. The Woolly Bugger is simply a Woolly Worm with a marabou tail added. You could guess that the term Woolly Worm came from the caterpillar-like appearance of this bushy fly. It would be interesting to know where the name Woolly Bugger came from (a Woolly Bug?). In some instances, the Woolly Worm is just as effective as the Wooly Bugger; for example, when tied with a black body and natural grizzly hackle the Wooly Worm resembles the salt-and-pepper colored dragonfly nymphs common to many lakes.

Fishing the Woolly Bugger

Woolly Buggers of various sizes and colors probably account for more big trout caught in streams and lakes than any other fly. A Wooly Bugger can simulate a baitfish, a crayfish, a dragonfly nymph, a leech, or maybe the trout just see it as lifelike prey. Fished with a floating line and cast back into the shoreline reeds where trout hide in lakes, a quickly retrieved Woolly Bugger will often bring a smashing strike. The same holds true for stream trout holding next to cover such as sunken brush, logs, bridge pilings, or anywhere large trout hide.

A simple but effective technique is to cast straight across the stream, then retrieve the Bugger with quick 6-inch pulls of the line. Fishing a Bugger is exciting because trout smack the scurrying fly hard. A sinktip line allows you to probe deeper for trout in streams and lakes because the fly sinks deeper after the cast and the sinktip keeps the fly down deeper on the retrieve. When fishing Woolly Buggers, before you change fly colors or sizes, try varying your retrieve, going from slow to medium to fast to super fast, and intersperse pauses. When fishing a lake in the middle of a hot summer day, try using a full sinking line and a Woolly Bugger to energize those lunkers taking a nap at the bottom. If that doesn't work, you can always take a nap, too.

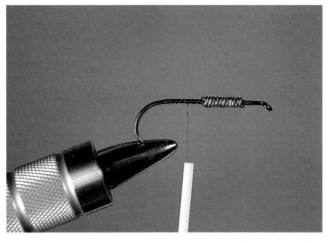

1) Debarb hook. Attach thread, wrap to rear of hook. Wrap lead wire around front half of hook, leaving room for head. Wrap thread forward through lead, then back to rear of lead wire.

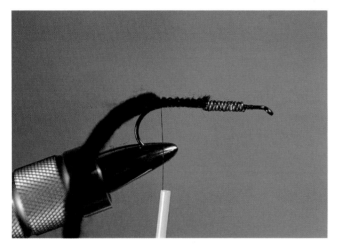

2) Tie in yarn where lead leaves off.

3) Tie in marabou and trim. (Marabou should be about hook shank length.)

4) Tie in hackle by tip, leaving room for one wrap of yarn behind hackle. Bring thread forward.

5) Wrap yarn forward, tie off and trim.

6) Wrap hackle forward, tie off and trim. Whip finish and cement head.

About the Author

Deke Meyer is a full time freelancer from Monmouth, Oregon, where he lives with his wife Barbara, who also fly fishes. He tied his first fly from a kit that arrived as a Christmas gift when he was 13 years old. His first size 10 fly had wings more suited for a size 6 fly. But with practice and working on the proper proportions, his flies got better and he caught fish. With the help of this book, and by remembering that fly tying is simply a matter of practice and proportion, you can tie flies that take trout, too.

His articles have been featured in most of the major fly fishing and outdoor magazines. His previous books include *Float Tube Fly Fishing, Advanced Fly Fishing For Steelhead,* and *Tying Trout Flies 12 of the Best,* by Frank Amato Publications.

If you have any comments or would like to write to the author, he can be reached through the publisher at the following address:

Deke Meyer c/o Frank Amato Publications
PO Box 82112
Portland, OR 97282